ᴅᴋ READERS

Level 3

Level 4

A Note to Parents

DK READERS is a compelling program for beginning readers, designed in conjunction with leading literacy experts, including Dr. Linda Gambrell, Director of the Eugene T. Moore School of Education at Clemson University. Dr. Gambrell has served on the Board of Directors of the International Reading Association and as President of the National Reading Conference.

Beautiful illustrations and superb full-color photographs combine with engaging, easy-to-read stories to offer a fresh approach to each subject in the series. Each DK READER is guaranteed to capture a child's interest while developing his or her reading skills, general knowledge, and love of reading.

The five levels of DK READERS are aimed at different reading abilities, enabling you to choose the books that are exactly right for your child:

Pre-level 1: Learning to read
Level 1: Beginning to read
Level 2: Beginning to read alone
Level 3: Reading alone
Level 4: Proficient readers

The "normal" age at which a child begins to read can be anywhere from three to eight years old, so these levels are only a general guideline.

No matter which level you select, you can be sure that you are helping your child learn to read, then read to learn!

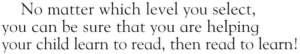

DK

LONDON, NEW YORK, MUNICH,
MELBOURNE, AND DELHI

Series Editor Deborah Lock
Art Editor Sadie Thomas
U.S. Editor John Searcy
DTP Designer Almudena Díaz
Production Alison Lenane
Picture Researcher Sarah Pownall
Jacket Designer Nina Tara
Illustrator Peter Dennis
Indexer Lynn Bresler
Reading Consultant
Linda Gambrell, Ph.D.

First American Edition, 2005
05 06 07 08 10 9 8 7 6 5 4 3 2 1
Published in the United States by DK Publishing, Inc.
375 Hudson Street, New York, New York 10014

Published in Great Britain by Dorling Kindersley Limited

Library of Congress Cataloging-in-Publication Data
Polin, C. J.
The story of chocolate / written by C. J. Polin.
-- 1st American ed.
p. cm.
ISBN 0-7566-0992-5 (pb) -- ISBN 0-7566-0991-7 (hc)
1. Chocolate--History. 2. Chocolate processing. I. Title.
TX791.P793 2005
641.3'374--dc22
2004015280

Color reproduction by Colourscan, Singapore
Printed and bound in China by L. Rex Printing Co. Ltd.

The publisher would like to thank the following for their kind
permission to reproduce their photographs.
a=above, b=below, c=center, l=left, r=right, t=top.
Jacket Images Front: Photolibrary.com: Paul Poplis.
The Advertising Archive: 45br. akg-images: 23t. **Alamy Images:** Andre Jenny
33b; G.P Bowater 36t. **The Art Archive:** Bodleian Library Oxford/The Bodleian
Library 15b; Dagli Orti 14b; Mireille Vautier 11c; Musee Bouilhet-Christofle
Paris/Dagli Orti 23b; Museo de America Madrid/Dagli Orti 13br.
www.bridgeman.co.uk: Museo de America, Madrid 18; The Stapleton Collection
15tr. **Chip Clark:** 6-7b(midge), 7tl, 34br. **Corbis:** 38b; Bettmann 22, 26, 47t; Bob
Krist 8t; Christine Osborne 25; Joe McDonald 33tr; Kevin Schafer 7r; Reuters 5c,
21. **DK Images:** Copyright CONCULTA-INAH-MEX. Authorized reproduction
by the Instituto Nacional de Antropologia e Historia. 11b; Copyright Judith Miller
& Dorling Kindersley/Noel Barrett Antique & Auctions House 27br; Copyright
Judith Miller & Dorling Kindersley/T W Conroy, NY. 43t. **Dolfin Chocolat:** 44.
Mary Evans Picture Library: 12, 29br. **Fairtrade Foundation:** 36br. **Getty
Images:** Angelo Cavalli 9; Juan Silva 43b. **Grenada Chocolate Company:** 39b.
Hulton Archive/Getty Images: Haywood Magee/Picture Post 32b. **Kobal
Collection:** Warner Bros 47br. **Lindt & Sprungli (International) AG:** 29c, 42t.
Lonely Planet Images: Greg Elms 46b. **N.H.P.A.:** Haroldo Palo Jr 10tl.
Photolibrary.com: Brian Hagiwara 28br. **Plamil Foods Ltd:** 35br. **Eric
Postpischil:** http://edp.org/Germany/Koeln.html/ Imhoff-Stollwerck-Museum 27tr,
31t. **Rex Features:** The Travel Library 4. **Karen Robinson:** 37. **Science Photo
Library:** Dr Morley Read 6l. **Earl Taylor:** Trade card from the private collection
of Earl Taylor, Dorchester, Massachusetts 24b. **Topfoto.co.uk:** 5br. **TransFair
USA:** 36bc. **Zefa Visual Media:** G.Baden 45c; Miep van Damm 28bl.
All other images © Dorling Kindersley Limited
For further information see: www.dkimages.com

Discover more at
www.dk.com

Contents

DK READERS

The Story of Chocolate

Written by C. J. Polin

DK Publishing, Inc.

Chocolate trees

Do you like chocolate? Most people would answer "Yes!" We eat an average of 11 pounds (5 kg) of chocolate per person per year. That's about 100 chocolate bars each! But where does chocolate come from, and how is it made into the sweet, delicious treats that we love to eat?

The story of chocolate begins in the rain forest, where cacao (ka-KOW) trees grow. Cocoa (KO-ko) pods grow on the cacao trees, and inside the pods are seeds called cocoa beans. These cocoa beans are the magic ingredient in chocolate.

Dried cocoa beans

Theobroma cacao

In 1753, Swedish scientist Linnaeus gave the cacao tree its scientific name, *Theobroma cacao*, meaning "food of the gods." It was well known that he liked chocolate!

Cacao trees grow in the hot, damp shade beneath the leafy canopy of the taller trees in the rain forest. There, the cacao trees blossom with pink and white flowers. Unlike on other trees, these flowers grow directly from the trunk and main branches. Tiny insects called gnats carry pollen between the blossoms, fertilizing them so cocoa pods will grow.

*A gnat sitting on
the tip of a pin.*

Only a fraction
of the hundreds
of blossoms
develop into
cocoa pods.
Like the blossoms, the
pods grow directly from
the trunk and branches
of the tree. Many cacao
trees grow both blossoms
and pods all year round.

After about four months, the cocoa pods grow to the size of melons. It takes another month before they are fully ripe. The color of the ripe pods ranges from yellow to dark red, depending on the tree. The pods are hard and must be split open with force to reveal the beans. Each pod contains about 40 cocoa beans surrounded by sticky white pulp. These are the precious beans that make chocolate.

Who first discovered that these strange-looking beans from these strange-looking trees could be used to make such a delicious treat?

An ancient treat

Cacao trees grow in the ancient area called Mesoamerica, which includes southern Mexico and Central America. Many experts believe that the first people to crack open a cocoa pod and use the bean were the ancient Olmec people, who lived from about 1200 to 200 B.C.E.

North America

South America

The three civilizations were in Mesoamerica.

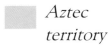
Aztec territory

Olmec territory

Mayan territory

The Mayan and Aztec civilizations followed. The Mayans were the first people to plant the beans of wild cacao trees. This was the beginning of cocoa farming.

In return for other goods, the Mayans traded cocoa beans to the Aztecs, whose lands were too dry to grow cacao trees.

Olmec monuments

Much of Mesoamerican culture is said to originate from the ancient Olmecs. In southern Mexico, they carved huge stone heads to praise their rulers.

Both the Mayans and Aztecs
used cocoa beans to make a drink
known as chocolatl. The beans
were dried and crushed, and then
mixed with water. The Mayans
drank chocolatl hot, while the
Aztecs drank it cold.

Often flavorings, such as chili or vanilla, were added. Nevertheless, the taste must have been very bitter. In fact, the word chocolatl is said to mean "bitter water."

Chili peppers

Vanilla pods

Chocolatl was served on special occasions, such as rituals and royal feasts. The mixture was usually poured from a height into the drinking vessel to make a thick foam on the top.

Both the Mayans and Aztecs used cocoa beans as money. They also gave beans as special gifts, and as offerings to the gods.

The land where cacao trees grew was very valuable. Over several centuries, the Aztecs expanded their empire and took over much of this land, including Mayan territories.

They collected taxes from the people in the form of cocoa beans. The Aztec kings filled storehouses with the precious beans. It is said that the emperor Montezuma had more than 960 million beans in his storehouses.

Emperor Montezuma

Army food supplies

Some of Montezuma's cocoa beans were made into wafers for his army. This was an early type of instant cocoa mix.

To Europe and beyond

In 1492, Christopher Columbus became the first European to sail to the Americas. During his fourth and final voyage to the New World in 1502, his ship came across a Mayan trading canoe full of cargo. Columbus ordered his crew to capture it.

Columbus's son, Ferdinand, wrote that among the loot taken from the canoe were "almonds." Ferdinand noticed that the Mayans treated them with great care. These "almonds" were, of course, cocoa beans. Although Columbus took some back to Spain, both he and the Spanish king were far too interested in gold and other treasures to take much notice of the small brown beans.

Other explorers soon followed Columbus to the New World. In 1519, Spanish explorer Hernando Cortés arrived in Mexico. The Aztec emperor, Montezuma, honored Cortés by serving him a feast with chocolatl to drink for dessert.

But Cortés had come to Mexico to claim the land for Spain, and by 1521 he had conquered the great Aztec nation. The Spanish explorers took on some Aztec customs, such as using cocoa beans as money. The taste of chocolatl was too bitter for them at first, but with the addition of sugar to sweeten the flavor, the exotic drink became a favorite treat.

Sugar cane

Molinillo (mole-i-NEE-yo)
The Spanish explorers used a mixing stick called a molinillo to whip up the thick foam on top of their hot chocolatl.

The explorers brought cocoa beans back to Spain and introduced the country to the hot, sweet drink that became known as chocolate. The drink soon became popular among the noble classes. Both cocoa beans and sugar had to be imported from the tropical rain forests in Central America, so chocolate was a luxury that only the rich could afford. Chocolate was also said to be good for your health, which increased demand.

Explorers from Spain were already busy in the New World, taking over land that was suitable for growing cacao trees. They could see that cocoa was going to be a money-making crop.

Since cocoa beans were in short supply, the Spanish did not want to share the delights of drinking chocolate. It took nearly 100 years for the secret to spread to other parts of Europe. There is a legend that English pirates captured a Spanish ship carrying cocoa beans. The pirates thought that the beans were sheep droppings and they burned them.

However, by the 1650s, Europeans were drinking chocolate at fashionable cafés called chocolate houses. In 1660, Princess Maria Teresa of Spain married King Louis XIV of France. Maria Teresa liked chocolate so much that she had a special maid to make it for her. Soon, the French nobles began copying their new queen, and developed a taste for the drink.

Chocolate pot

Tea from Asia and coffee from Africa were also popular in Europe at this time. Special pitchers, such as this chocolate pot, were used to serve each drink.

Cocoa powder

By the 1700s, European settlers had brought the chocolate drink back across the Atlantic Ocean, where it became a popular treat in the colonies of North America.

In 1765, the first American chocolate factory opened in Massachussetts.

WALTER BAKER & CO'S MILLS - DORCHESTER, MASS.

John Hannon had run a chocolate business in Ireland. While looking for work after arriving in America, he met Dr. James Baker, who suggested going into business together. Their new chocolate factory had a waterwheel that powered a machine, which ground the cocoa beans into a fine powder. Until then, most cocoa powder had been handmade.

Chocolate factories

In 1765, Scottish inventor James Watt built a steam engine that made goods quickly and cheaply. Using a steam-powered chocolate grinder made chocolate a cheaper treat for everyone.

James Watt studying a steam engine

In 1828, Dutch chemist Coenraad van Houten invented a chocolate press that made the

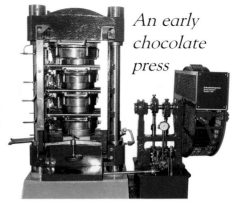

An early chocolate press

chocolate taste better, too. Cocoa beans are made up of the meat of the bean, called cocoa mass, and fatty cocoa butter. Cocoa butter gave chocolate a greasy texture and didn't mix well with water. The chocolate press separated out much of the cocoa butter. The result was chocolate that had a purer flavor and mixed easily with water.

The age of steam

Watt's steam engine led to the development of new machines, including the steam-powered fire pumper. It started the Industrial Revolution.

In the 1840s, Fry's chocolate company in England made the first solid chocolate for eating when they mixed cocoa powder and sugar with melted cocoa butter instead of water. The new mixture was poured into a mold and then cooled so the chocolate would harden.

The chocolate business boomed. Many different kinds of chocolate for eating were molded into bars and other shapes—some were even filled with flavored centers.

Chocolate was now cheaper for everyone, and sold to people of all ages. Cadbury's, another English company, made boxes of different chocolates that were decorated with pictures, which children could cut out and keep. Chocolate was thought to be a healthy and delicious treat.

Chocolate was advertised as a healthy treat.

New towns
In England, Cadbury's and Rowntree's chocolate companies were run by Quaker families, who took good care of their workers and built new towns for them.

Until 1875, all chocolate had been what we now call plain or dark chocolate. It was also coarse and gritty. Then, two separate developments happened in Switzerland.

Henri Nestlé was experimenting with condensed milk for breakfast cereals when his partner, Daniel Peter, suggested adding condensed milk to chocolate. By doing this, they invented milk chocolate.

Four years later,
Rudolphe Lindt invented
the "conche," a machine
with rollers that moved
back and forth over
the chocolate.

Cocoa mass

Model of
Lindt's
conche
machine

The movement created
friction and heat that
broke down even
the tiniest crumbs.
The result was chocolate
with a smooth, velvety
texture.

In the United States, Milton Hershey opened his chocolate factory in 1905. Hershey built his factory in the dairy region of Pennsylvania, where he could easily get a large supply of milk. Using th latest technology, he mass-produced milk chocolate candies. One of his early successes was Hershey's Milk Chocolate with Almonds, which is still a bestseller.

Hershey built a large, modern town for his workers, with a hotel for visitors, a golf course, and other recreational facilities. Over the years, tourism has increased, and the site has expanded into an amusement park. The town of Hershey has streets called Cocoa Avenue and Chocolate Avenue, and streetlamps shaped like Hershey's Kisses, one of the company's most popular products.

Making chocolate today

The average cacao tree only produces about 2 pounds (1 kg) of dried cocoa beans. More and more land is being taken over by cacao-tree growers to meet the huge demand for chocolate. Cacao trees now grow on plantations in many tropical rain forests within 20 degrees of the Equator. They need a hot, wet climate, low altitude, and lots of gnats to pollinate the blossoms.

North America

Central America

South America

Area where cacao trees are grown

Cacao trees are usually planted among taller trees, such as banana or coconut trees, which give them the shade they need. After about four years, pods begin growing on a young cacao tree.

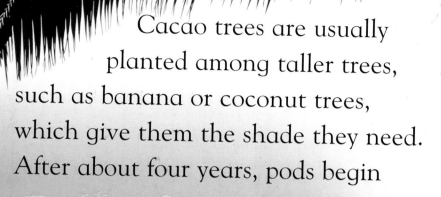

Europe

Asia

20°N

Africa

Equator

20°S

Australia

Organic chocolate

On some small farms, pesticides are not used and cacao trees are grown with native plants, which helps the environment. This chocolate is labeled "organic."

Despite the progress in making chocolate, cocoa farming must still be done by hand, as it was by the Mayans and Aztecs. Workers use knives to cut the ripe pods off the trees—being careful not to damage the bark. Then, they split the pods open with wooden mallets and remove the cocoa beans and the sticky white pulp.

Fair trade

Chocolate that is labeled "fair trade" guarantees farmers a fair price for their cocoa beans. The label differs between countries, but the message is the same.

FAIR TRADE
CERTIFIED™
USA

FAIRTRADE
Guarantees
a **better deal**
for Third World
Producers
UK

The beans and the pulp are heaped into big piles to ferment—a natural process that helps bring out the flavor. After fermenting for about a week, the beans are dried in the sun and shipped to the chocolate factories.

At the factory, the beans are cleaned and then roasted at a very high temperature to bring out their flavor.

A hulling machine then separates the shell from the inside of the bean, which is called the "nib."

The roasting machine

Cooking with cocoa

Cocoa powder is often used as an ingredient in other foods, such as cookies, cake, and ice cream.

Only the nib of the bean is used to make chocolate. The nibs are ground in a machine until they turn into a thick paste. This paste is then pressed to separate the fatty cocoa butter from the cocoa mass.

To make cocoa powder, the cocoa mass is ground again into a fine powder. For chocolate-drink mixes, sugar is added to the cocoa powder.

The grinding machine

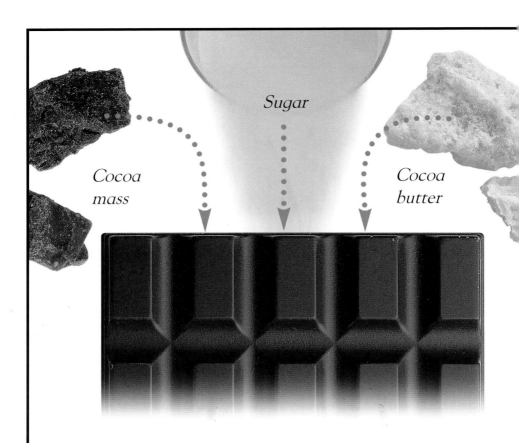

Cocoa mass

Sugar

Cocoa butter

Dark chocolate is cocoa mass mixed with sugar and some melted cocoa butter. The mixture is ground up and then put into a conche machine, where the rollers make the chocolate smooth. Then it is cooled in a process called "tempering" to give it the ideal texture.

To make milk chocolate, milk and sugar are mixed and heated, so that much of the liquid evaporates. This condensed milk is mixed with cocoa mass and dried into a crumbly mixture, which is then ground up and mixed with cocoa butter (often diluted with vegetable fat). Once flavorings such as vanilla have been added, the milk chocolate is conched and tempered.

Milk chocolate

Dark chocolate

White chocolate

White chocolate contains sugar, milk, and cocoa butter, but no cocoa mass. Technically, it is not real chocolate.

Assembly line of chocolate bars

Many chocolate bars are still made in molds, but these days, the molds are usually filled by machines. Some machines can fill more than 1,000 molds in a minute—making this same number of bars! Nuts, caramel, and other ingredients can also be added during the molding process. Then, the bars go through a cooling tunnel so the chocolate can harden.

Chocolate is also used as a covering for cookies, ice cream, and cake. The filling is dipped or squirted with chocolate until it is covered. This process is called "enrobing."

The next time you buy a chocolate bar, read the label before making your choice—the purer the chocolate, the better the bar.

These French chocolate bars show the percentage of cocoa solids.

On most labels, cocoa mass and cocoa butter are measured together and called "cocoa solids." The percentage of cocoa solids in chocolate varies from about 15 to 75 percent. Dark chocolate usually contains more cocoa solids than milk chocolate.

Modern chocolate has a bad reputation when it comes to nutrition. However, many experts now agree that cocoa solids may be good for you, and that it is the sugar and other added ingredients that are fattening and unhealthy. It depends what kind of chocolate— and how much of it— you eat.

Soldiers' rations

During World War II, much of the chocolate produced in the U.S. was given to the soldiers for nourishment and strength as part of their daily rations.

CHOCOLATE IS A *Fighting* FOOD !

All kinds of chocolate

Today, there are many different kinds of chocolate treats—bars, cookies, cake, ice cream, and many others.

In Mexico, where the cacao tree was first discovered, a popular dish is a chocolate-chili sauce called molé poblano (mole-ay puh-BLAH-noh). It is made with plain chocolate and often eaten with chicken or turkey.

Molé poblano has a rich and spicy taste.

Chefs pouring chocolate into a 7-feet (2.1-m) tall and 5-inches (12.7-cm) deep heart-shaped mold.

Some chocolate creations are truly enormous! One record-breaking treat weighed 15,400 pounds (7,000 kg)—as much as 140,000 chocolate bars. But, like all chocolate, it began with a pod full of beans.

A sweet read

Roald Dahl was inspired by his childhood experiences as a taste tester in a candy factory when writing his book *Charlie and the Chocolate Factory*.

Glossary

Cacao tree
The tree on which cocoa pods grow.

Chocolate press
A machine that squeezes the cocoa butter out of the chocolate, leaving the cocoa mass.

Chocolatl
The name used by the Mayans and Aztecs for their chocolate drink.

Cocoa beans
The seeds inside the cocoa pods that are used to make chocolate.

Cocoa butter
The fatty substance that is found in cocoa beans.

Cocoa mass
The part of chocolate that is left after the cocoa butter has been separated out.

Cocoa pods
The fruit of the cacao tree.

Cocoa solids
Cocoa mass and cocoa butter measured together.

Conche
A machine with rollers that heat and crush the crumbly chocolate mixture to make it smooth.

Condensed milk
Milk that has been heated so that much of the liquid evaporates.

Dark chocolate
Also known as plain chocolate, it is made of cocoa mass, cocoa butter, and sugar.

Enrobing
Covering a food such as ice cream, cake, or cookies with chocolate.

Fermentation
A natural process by which the cocoa beans break down, making the chocolate flavor stronger.

Gnats
Small flying insects that carry pollen between the blossoms on the cacao tree. They pollinate the flowers, allowing the pods to grow.

Hulling
To separate the nib from the bean shell.

Mesoamerica
Historic area of what is now Mexico and Central America, where the Olmecs, Mayans, and Aztecs lived.

Milk chocolate
Chocolate to which milk has been added during manufacturing.

Nib
The inside of the cocoa bean, after the shell has been removed.

Pulp
The soft part of a fruit. In a cocoa pod, sticky white pulp covers the cocoa beans.

Rain forest
A thick forest area where the climate is hot and damp.

Tempering
Manufacturing process in which chocolate is carefully cooled to give it the right texture.

Index